WRESTLING SUPERSTARS

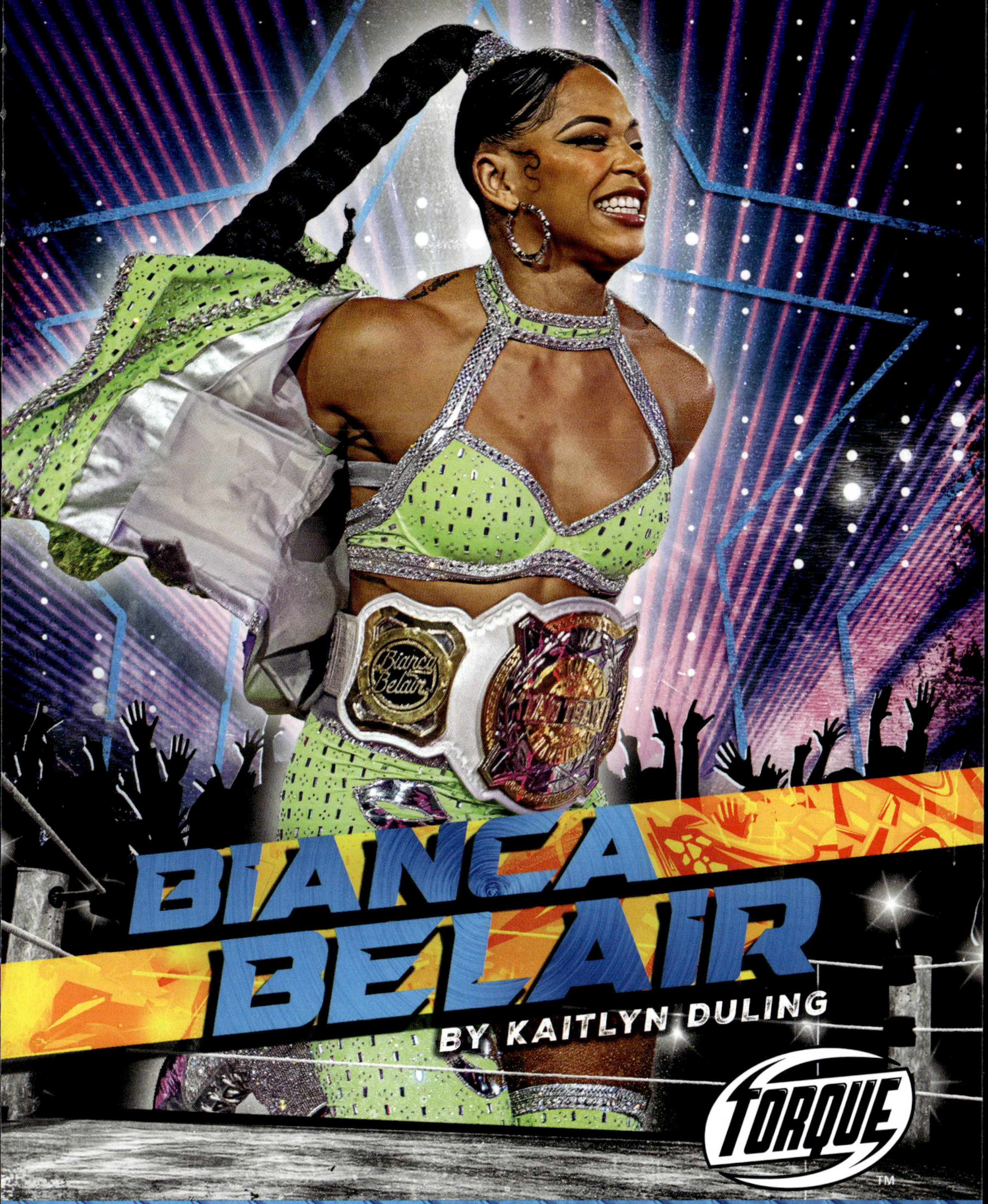

BIANCA BELAIR

BY KAITLYN DULING

TORQUE™

TORQUE, AN IMPRINT OF BELLWETHER MEDIA BY FLUTTERBEE

TORQUE™

Torque brims with excitement perfect for thrill-seekers of all kinds. Discover daring survival skills, explore uncharted worlds, and marvel at mighty engines and extreme sports. In *Torque* books, anything can happen. Are you ready?

This edition first published in 2027 by Bellwether Media, Inc.

For information regarding permission, write to Bellwether Media, Inc., Attention: Permissions Department, 3500 American Blvd W, Suite 150, Bloomington, MN 55431.

Library of Congress Cataloging-in-Publication Data

Names: Duling, Kaitlyn author
Title: Bianca Belair / by Kaitlyn Duling.
Description: Torque. | Minneapolis, Minnesota : Bellwether Media, Inc, [2027] | Series: Wrestling superstars | Includes bibliographical references and index. | Audience: Ages 8-12 | Audience: Grades 4-6 | Summary: "Engaging imagesaccompany information about Bianca Belair. The combination of high-interest subject matter and light text is intended for students in grades 3 through 7" – Provided by publisher.
Identifiers: LCCN 2026010722 (print) | LCCN 2026010723 (ebook) | ISBN 9798898801083 library binding | ISBN 9798898802325 ebook
Subjects: LCSH: Belair, Bianca, 1989- | Women wrestlers–United States | World Wrestling Entertainment, Inc. | LCGFT: Biographies | Juvenile literature
Classification: LCC GV1196.B44 D85 2027 (print) | LCC GV1196.B44 (ebook) | DDC 796.812092 [B] -dc23/eng/20260217
LC record available at https://lccn.loc.gov/2026010722
LC ebook record available at https://lccn.loc.gov/2026010723

ISBN: 9798898801083 (hardcover)
ISBN: 9798898802325 (ebook)

Editor: Suzane Nguyen   Series Designer: Gabriel Hilger

Printed in the United States of America, North Mankato, MN.

TABLE OF CONTENTS

A SURPRISE MOVE

It is WrestleMania 38. The crowd is quiet. Bianca Belair is on the mat. Becky Lynch is close to winning. Is it over for Belair?

No! Belair jumps onto the ropes. She does a backflip. Then she picks up Lynch. Belair slams her down. The crowd goes wild. Belair is the strongest tonight. She is the Raw Women's Champion!

WHO IS BIANCA BELAIR?

Bianca Belair is a wrestler in **World Wrestling Entertainment (WWE)**. She once held the WWE Raw Women's Championship **title** for more than 400 days! That is longer than any other female wrestler.

BIANCA BELAIR

BIRTHDAY
APRIL 9, 1989

HOMETOWN
KNOXVILLE, TENNESSEE

COMPANY
WWE

HEIGHT
5'7"

THEME SONG

"Watch Me Shine"
CFO$, Nicole Tranquillo

Belair is known for her strength and her long braid. She uses it as a weapon! She sews all the wrestling **gear** she wears.

FROM THE TRACK TO THE MAT

BELAIR'S MOTHER'S GODFATHER Z. ALEXANDER LOOBY

MAKING HISTORY

Some of Belair's family members were part of the civil rights movement. They fought for equal rights.

Belair grew up in Knoxville, Tennessee. She had many leaders in her family.

As a child, Belair was always active. Her parents saw this and signed her up for sports. Belair did track and field when she was four. In high school, she set **records** in **hurdles**. She won many awards!

Belair ran track and field at three colleges. After college, she started to compete in **powerlifting**. Fans of the sport started to follow her online.

Belair trained too hard and hurt her rib. She decided to quit powerlifting. She worked for a company doing phone sales. Belair thought her days as a star were over.

FAVORITES

HAIRSTYLE
LONG BRAID

FOOD
BAKED MACARONI AND CHEESE

NON-WRESTLING SPORT
TRACK AND FIELD

GEAR
ROSE GEAR
(WRESTLEMANIA 41)

THE EST OF WWE

NAME GAME

Belair's nickname is The EST of WWE. It means she is the fastest, strongest, roughest, greatest, and the best!

TIMELINE

2016

Belair signs with WWE

2018

Belair marries fellow wrestler Montez Ford

In 2015, former WWE wrestler Mark Henry sent Belair a message. He had seen her powerlifting videos. He wanted her to try out for WWE! Belair agreed. After two tryouts, she was in!

Belair signed a **contract** with WWE in 2016. She started out as a **heel** named Binky Blair. In 2017, she changed her name to Bianca Belair.

2020

Belair joins the WWE main roster

2023

Belair becomes the longest-reigning Raw Women's Champion

2024

Belair becomes a WWE Women's Triple Crown Champion

BELAIR AND MONTEZ FORD

In 2020, Belair joined the WWE main **roster**. She made her **debut** at WrestleMania 36 as a **face**. She helped save Montez Ford and Angelo Dawkins from three other wrestlers.

In 2021, Belair became the first Black female wrestler to win a Royal Rumble. Later that year, she wrestled in a 5-on-5 **match**. Belair was the last wrestler standing!

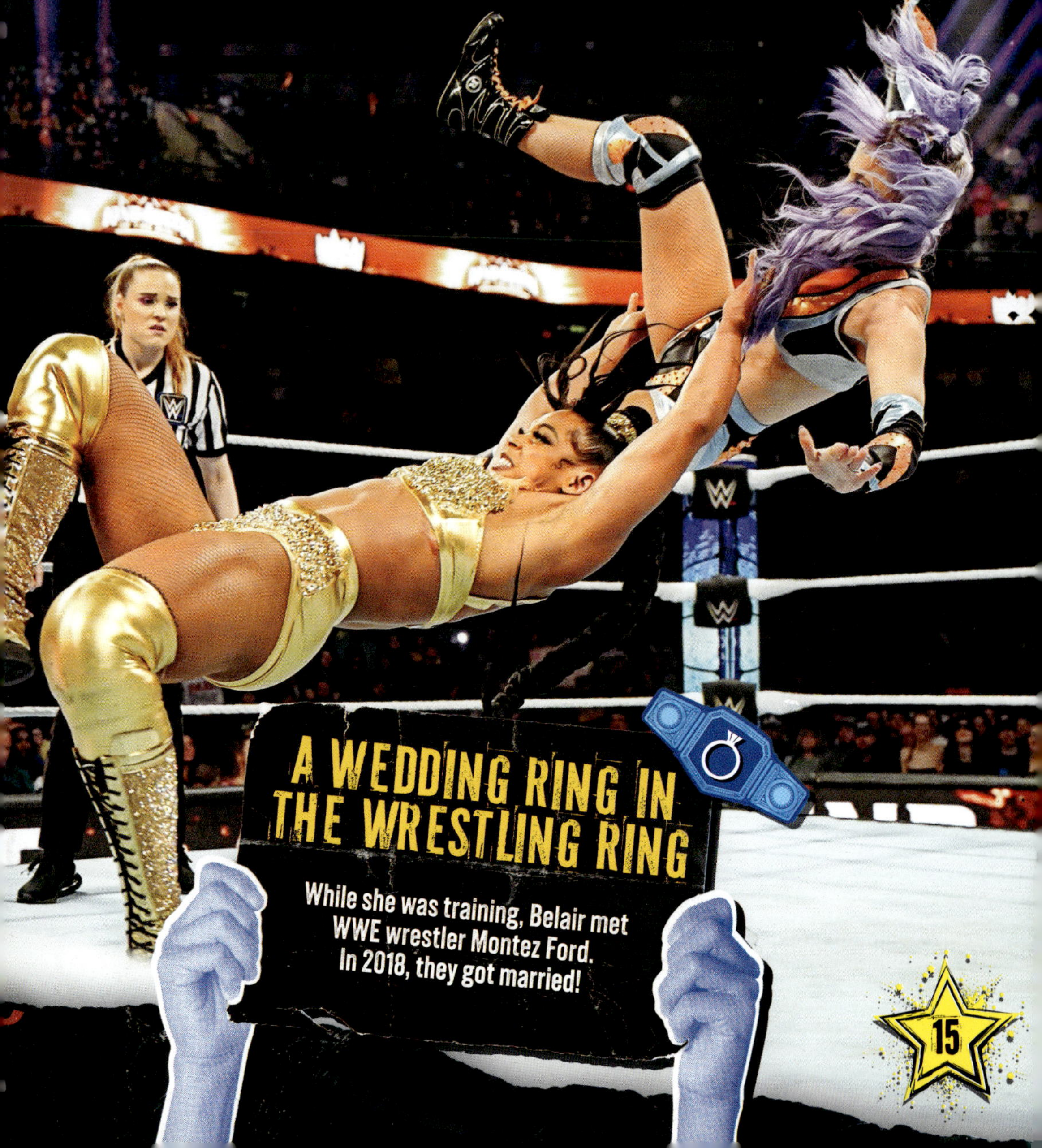

A WEDDING RING IN THE WRESTLING RING

While she was training, Belair met WWE wrestler Montez Ford. In 2018, they got married!

At WrestleMania 37 in 2021, Belair won her first WWE SmackDown Women's Championship. In 2022, she fought against Becky Lynch during WrestleMania 38. Belair won and became the WWE Raw Women's Champion!

From April 2022 to May 2023, Belair was the WWE Women's World Champion. She was the champion for 420 days. It set a record!

WRESTLEMANIA 37

1, 2, 3!

Belair has won a SmackDown Championship, a Raw Championship, and a Tag Team Championship. That makes her a WWE Women's Triple Crown Champion!

TITLES

as of 2025

2X WWE RAW (NOW WWE) WOMEN'S CHAMPION

1 WWE SMACKDOWN WOMEN'S CHAMPION

2X WWE WOMEN'S TAG TEAM CHAMPION

1 WWE ROYAL RUMBLE WINNER

Belair joined two **tag teams** in 2024. She teamed up with Jade Cargill and Naomi. She won the WWE Women's Tag Team Championship twice that year.

At WrestleMania 41, Belair fought Iyo Sky and Rhea Ripley. It was a huge match! She did not win, but she fought hard. A broken finger meant she had to take a break from wrestling.

TOP MOVES

K.O.D.
(KISS OF DEATH)

FLIPS THE OPPONENT FROM HER SHOULDERS, SLAMMING THEM INTO THE MAT FACE-FIRST

HAIR WHIP

SMACKS THE OPPONENT WITH HER BRAID

POWERSLAM

THROWS THE OPPONENT TO THE MAT AND THEN FALLS FACE DOWN ON TOP OF THEM

TIME FOR A TURN

Outside of wrestling, Belair has been busy. In 2020, WWE created a Bianca Belair **action figure**! She has a TV show with her husband. Belair has also been in many video games, including *Fortnite*.

FUTURE MOVIE STAR

In 2025, Belair signed a contract with an acting company. She hopes to act in movies like Dwayne "the Rock" Johnson, John Cena, and other wrestling superstars.

Fans are wondering if Belair will turn heel. Who knows what is next for the EST of WWE!

GLOSSARY

action figure—a posable plastic toy figurine that looks like a person or character

contract—an official agreement

debut—a person's first appearance or performance

face—a hero character

gear—the clothes a wrestler wears in the ring

heel—a villain character

hurdles—a sport where people run and jump over barriers

match—a contest between wrestlers

powerlifting—a sport where people do different types of weightlifting

records—titles a wrestler holds longer than any other wrestler

roster—a list of participants in wrestling

tag teams—pairs or groups of wrestlers who wrestle as a team

title—the status of being the champion

World Wrestling Entertainment (WWE)—the world's largest professional wrestling and sports entertainment company

TO LEARN MORE

AT THE LIBRARY

Duling, Kaitlyn. *Rhea Ripley*. Minneapolis, Minn.: Bellwether Media, 2027.

Leed, Percy. *Pro Wrestling Superstars*. Minneapolis, Minn.: Lerner Publications, 2025.

Tischler, Joe. *Bianca Belair*. Mankato, Minn.: Amicus Learning, 2025.

ON THE WEB

FACTSURFER

Factsurfer.com gives you a safe, fun way to find more information.

1. Go to www.factsurfer.com
2. Enter "Bianca Belair" into the search box and click 🔍.
3. Select your book cover to see a list of related content.

INDEX

The images in this book are reproduced through the courtesy of: Diego Serrano/ Wikimedia Commons, front cover; WWE/ Contributor/ Getty Images, pp. 3, 4, 5 (top, bottom), 6, 7, 9, 10, 11 (hairstyle, Bianca Belair), 12, 14 (top), 15, 17, 18, 19 (all), 20, 21, 22; WikiLeon/ Wikimedia Commons, p. 5 (championship belt); Everett Collection Inc/ Alamy Stock Photo, p. 8; Magrig, p. 11 (baked macaroni and cheese); Maria, p. 11 (track and field); Ethan Miller/ Staff/ Getty Images, p. 11 (rose gear); Alex Bierens de Haan/ Stringer/ Getty Images, p. 13 (2023); lev radin, p. 14 (bottom); ZUMA Press Inc/ Alamy Stock Photo, p. 16.